POCKET
KARDASHIAN
WISDOM

POCKET

KARDASHIAN

wisdom

SASSY, SHAMELESS AND SURPRISINGLY
PROFOUND QUOTES FROM THE WHOLE FAMILY

Hardie Grant

BOOKS

CONTENTS

STYLE

'I BELIEVE THAT, NO MATTER HOW OLD YOU ARE, A WOMAN CAN LOOK AMAZING.'

Kris

On breaking up with Scott:

'LET'S LOOK ON THE BRIGHT SIDE, NOW I HAVE A HUGE CLOSET GUYS.'

Kourtney

On pregnancy:

'I THINK GOD WAS DOING THIS FOR A REASON. HE WAS SAYING: "KIM, YOU THINK YOU'RE SO HOT, BUT LOOK WHAT I CAN DO TO YOU."'

Kim

'IF I POST THE WRONG SELFIE, THEN I AM LIKE "UGH, THAT OTHER SELFIE WAS SO MUCH BETTER THAN THAT SELFIE," BUT OTHER THAN THAT I DON'T REALLY REGRET ANYTHING.'

Kylie

'I'LL CRY AT THE END OF THE DAY. NOT WITH FRESH MAKE UP.'

Kim

'I ONLY JUST STARTED WEARING UNDERWEAR A MONTH AGO.'

Kim

'I LOVE LONG NAILS. THEY GIVE ME ENERGY.'

Khloé

'THE KEY TO A GOOD SELFIE IS LIGHTING. IF YOU'RE NOT FEELING YOURSELF, MAKE IT DARKER.'

Kim

Jewellery salesperson:

'42 CARATS.
$1.2 MILLION.'

Kim:

'THAT'S NOT SO BAD.'

'I CHANGE MY STYLE MAYBE EVERY MONTH. I'M, LIKE, PUNK ONE MONTH, GHETTO FAB THE NEXT, CLASSY THE NEXT. I'M JUST YOUNG AND FINDING OUT WHO I AM.'

Kylie

On two-year-old North's style:

'SHE DOESN'T LIKE PINK OR PURPLE. SHE LIKES GREYS, CREAMS, OATMEAL COLOURS AND BLACK.'

Kim

HUSTLE

'UNLESS YOU'RE WILLING TO WORK REALLY, REALLY HARD, IT'S NEVER GOING TO HAPPEN.'

Kris

'I'M KYLIE
FUCKING JENNER.'

Kylie

'I DON'T HAVE CELL SERVICE HERE, AND IT'S MAKING ME HAVE A RASH.'

Kris

'WE'VE ALWAYS BEEN ABOUT THE BUSINESS.'

Kim

On how to feel sexy:

'HONESTLY, JUST BEING CONFIDENT IN YOURSELF AND BEING THE BOSS THAT YOU ARE.'

Kendall

Kris:

'I THINK KIM SHOULD DO *PLAYBOY*.'

Kourtney:

'OF COURSE YOU WANT HER TO DO IT, WITH YOUR 10% MANAGER COMMISSION. I KNOW ABOUT YOU.'

'IF SOMEBODY SAYS "NO", YOU'RE ASKING THE WRONG PERSON.'

Kris

Kris:

'YOU CAN'T ALWAYS GET WHAT YOU WANT.'

Khloé:

'EW.'

'I LOVE THE CREATIVE PROCESS AND BEING ABLE TO BUILD SOMETHING OUT OF NOTHING.'

Kris

'WE'VE RENTED OUT VERSAILLES.'

Kim

'WE HAVE LITERALLY MILLIONS AND MILLIONS OF FANS.'

Kris

SELF-LOVE

CHAPTER 3

Scott:

'YOU'RE BLOCKING MY VIEW.'

Kourtney:

'I AM THE VIEW.'

'DO YOUR SQUATS, EAT YOUR VEGETABLES, WEAR RED LIPSTICK, DON'T LET BOYS BE MEAN TO YOU.'

Kendall

'IF YOU'RE DIFFERENT,
OR IF YOU THINK SOMETHING
ABOUT YOU IS JUST WEIRD
AND OUT OF THE ORDINARY, I
JUST THINK THAT'S SO DOPE.'

Kylie

On whether she has any tattoos:

'HONEY, WOULD YOU PUT A BUMPER STICKER ON A BENTLEY?'

Kim

'KNOWING YOU'RE A BADASS BITCH IS JUST WHAT LIFE IS ABOUT.'

Khloé

Kourtney:

'I'M IN LOVE.'

Khloé:

'WITH WHO?'

Kourtney:

'MYSELF.'

'OUR FEELINGS ARE OUR FEELINGS.'

Kris

'EVERYBODY'S BEAUTIFUL.'

Kendall

'I THINK ALL DIETS
ARE KIND OF WEIRD.
THE WORD "DIE"
IS IN IT.'

Khloé

'MY VIBE RIGHT NOW IS JUST LIVING LIFE.'

Kourtney

'I LOVE WHERE MY EYEBROWS ARE GOING RIGHT NOW.'

Kim

HATERS

CHAPTER 4

'IF YOU'RE NOT INTO WHAT I'M POSTING, DON'T LOOK.'

Kim

'ON THE COVER OF A MAGAZINE IT SAID I WAS DRUNK AND ALONE AND JUST FOR THE RECORD, IS THERE A PROBLEM WITH THAT?'

Kris

'I LOVE IT WHEN PEOPLE UNDERESTIMATE ME AND THEN BECOME PLEASANTLY SURPRISED.'

Kim

'IT'S ALMOST, LIKE, *TRENDY* TO HATE ON MY FAMILY.'

Kendall

'BITCH, YOU DON'T KNOW ME.'

Kylie

'HONEY, I COULD CARE LESS.'

Kourtney

'I'VE NEVER CLAIMED TO BE ANYTHING THAT I'M NOT.'

Kim

'LIFE IS TOO SHORT TO BE WITH PEOPLE WHO DON'T HAVE GOOD ENERGY.'

Kris

'EVER SINCE KIM CALLED ME A TROLL, I LOVE USING THAT WORD.'

Khloé

'IT'S YOUR LIFE. IT'S NOT ABOUT WHAT OTHER PEOPLE THINK.'

Kourtney

'THERE ARE ALWAYS
GOING TO BE KIDS WHO ARE
MEAN BUT THE PEOPLE THAT
MATTER TO YOU — THE PEOPLE
YOU LOVE…THOSE ARE
THE PEOPLE YOU SHOULD
LISTEN TO.'

Kendall

FAMILY

CHAPTER 5

To Kylie, before giving birth:

'I NEED TO SCHOOL YOU ON WHAT YOUR VAGINA IS ABOUT TO FEEL LIKE. LIKE, FOR REAL.'

Kim

'MY MOM CURSED
SO MUCH WHEN
WE WERE LITTLE,
I THOUGHT MY NAME
WAS "FUCK".'

Khloé

Picking up the phone to Kris:

'YES, SATAN?'

Khloé

'WHEN YOU DATE ONE OF US, YOU KIND OF DATE THE WHOLE FAMILY.'

Kim

'YOU HAVE TO LIKE ME, I GAVE BIRTH TO YOU.'

Kris

'KIM, WOULD YOU STOP TAKING PICTURES OF YOURSELF, YOUR SISTER'S GOING TO JAIL.'

Kris

'THERE'S A LOT OF BAGGAGE THAT COMES WITH US, BUT IT'S LIKE LOUIS VUITTON BAGGAGE — YOU ALWAYS WANT IT.'

Kim

'WE MADE A PACT
AS A FAMILY AND SAID WE
WOULD BE TRULY AUTHENTIC
BECAUSE PEOPLE DON'T
BUY BULLSHIT.'

Kim

To Kris:

'YOU SHOULD BE HAPPY YOUR DAUGHTER HAS AN EDUCATION. ESPECIALLY SEX-ED. YOU OBVIOUSLY DIDN'T. THAT'S WHY YOU HAVE MULTIPLE BABY DADDIES AND THOUSANDS OF CHILDREN.'

Khloé

'YOU'RE ACTING LIKE DRUNK SLOB-KABOBS.'

Kourtney

'WHEN I'M, LIKE, 30,
I WANT TO GO OFF THE MAP,
HAVE A FAMILY AND LIVE
IN MALIBU WITH A FARM,
AND JUST RAISE MY
OWN CHICKENS.'

Kylie

SASS

CHAPTER 6

Kourtney:

'WHY DID YOU MAKE A SEX TAPE?'

Kim:

'BECAUSE I WAS HORNY AND I FELT LIKE IT.'

'YOU'RE NOT SPECIAL. SORRY.'

Kim

'I LEGIT DON'T CARE.'

Kylie

'EVERYTHING YOU'RE SAYING IS GOING IN ONE EAR AND OUT THE OTHER.'

Kourtney

Kourtney:

'QUEEN KOURTNEY IS WHAT THEY CALL ME.'

Khloé:

'WHO CALLS YOU THE QUEEN?'

Kourtney:

'EVERY SINGLE PERSON ON INSTAGRAM, TWITTER, AND ANYONE THAT MEETS ME.'

'ABCDEFG I HAVE TO GO. IT'S JUST A PHRASE I LIKE TO USE. IT MEANS THE CONVERSATION IS OVER.'

Kourtney

On allegations that Kim's marriage
to Kris Humphries was a publicity stunt:

'I THINK IF SHE WAS GOING TO DO IT FOR PUBLICITY, SHE'D PICK SOMEONE THAT PEOPLE KNEW.'

Kourtney

Khloé:

'KIM, YOU LOOK LIKE SUCH A LADY TODAY!'

Kim:

'REALLY? I WAS TRYING TO BE A WHORE.'

'THAT'S SO EMBARRASSING FOR YOUR LIFE. AND YOUR SOUL.'

Kourtney

'CAN I GET AN AMEN UP IN THIS BITCH?'

Khloé

Khloé:

'EVERYONE MAKES MISTAKES. ARE YOU THAT PERFECT THAT YOU CAN'T ACCEPT IT?'

Kourtney:

'OBVIOUSLY.'

Kim:

'MY DIAMOND EARRING CAME OFF IN THE OCEAN AND IT'S GONE!'

Kourtney:

'KIM, THERE'S PEOPLE THAT ARE DYING.'

'IN FIRST GRADE,
I TOLD MY FRIENDS I
HAD A THIRD STORY IN
MY HOUSE FILLED WITH
JEWELS AND LIONS.'

Kendall

'I'M SORRY YOU'RE OVERWHELMED.'

Kris

'EVERY TIME I GET OLDER, I LOOK BETTER AND GET SMARTER.'

Kourtney

'EXCLUSIVE: Kylie Jenner on her Racy Social Media Posts: 'I Don't Really Regret Anything', *Entertainment Tonight*, www.youtube.com – p. **11**

'The most relatable thing Kris Jenner has ever said', SeeBelieve, 2017, www.youtube.com – p. **51**

'Fitzy and Wippa Chat with Khloe Kardashian', *Fitzy and Wippa*, Nova 96.9, www.nova969.com.au – p. **45**

'Kim: "It Bothers Me That Im [sic] Not Pregnant", 2015, *ELLE* magazine (online), www.elle.com – p. **10**

'Kim and Khloe Kardashian on *The Wendy Williams Show*', 2009, *The Wendy Williams Show* – p. **39**

'Kylie Jenner talks bullying' [Youtube video], 2015, *ELLE* Canada, www.youtube.com – p. **38**

'"Pose in your underwear" and 12 other pieces of life advice from Kendall Jenner', 2017, *The Telegraph* (online), www.telegraph.co.uk – p. **27**, p. **37**, p. **61**

'To Our Daughter' [video], 2018, Kylie, www.youtube.com – p. **64**

Bennetts, L. 2011, 'Kim Kardashian: The 35 Million Dollar Baby', *Marie Claire* (online), www.marieclaire.com – p. **72**

Brodesser-Akner, T. 2015, 'Where Would the Kardashians Be Without Kris Jenner?', *The New York Times Magazine* (online), www.nytimes.com – p. **22**

Clements, E. 2013, 'Kendall Jenner & Kylie Jenner Talk Dating Deal-Breakers, Athletic Ability For *HuffPost*'s #nofilter', *Huffington Post*, www.huffingtonpost.co.uk – p. **91**

Curran, A. 2016, 'The Best Kylie Jenner Quotes For Every Social Situation', Buzznet, www.buzznet.com – p. **55**

Gavilanes, G. 2018, 'Read Her Lips: Kylie Jenner Doesn't *Want* to Be Famous – Here's How We Know', *People* (online), www.people.com – p. **23**

Jenner, K. 2012, *Kris Jenner... and All Things Kardashian*, Simon & Schuster – p. **29**

Keeping Up with the Kardashians, Seasons 1–15, E! – p. **9**, p. **13**, p. **15**, p. **17**, p. **24**, p. **28**, p. **30**, p. **32**, p. **36**, p. **41**, p. **42**, p. **43**, p. **44**, p. **46**, p. **47**, p. **50**, p. **56**, p. **59**, p. **60**, p. **61**, p. **65**, p. **66**, p. **67**, p. **69**, p. **70**, p. **71**, p. **73**, p. **74**, p. **78**, p. **79**, p. **80**, p. **81**, p. **82**, p. **83**, p. **85**, p. **87**, p. **88**, p. **89**, p. **90**, p. **92**, p. **93**

L. DePaulo. 2016, 'Kris Jenner: Target Practice', *Harper's Bazaar* (online), www.harpersbazaar.com – p. **33**

Lombardo, M. 2015, 'Kris Jenner: The Empress of Power', *Haute Living* (online), www.hauteliving.com – p. **8**, p. **31**, p. **58**

Morgan, P, 2014, 'PIERS MORGAN: The snobs can all kiss Kim's butt, her biggest talent is always being herself – and I love her for it!', *Daily Mail* (online), www.dailymail.co.uk – p. **25**

Pocket Kim Wisdom, 2016, Hardie Grant Books – p. **14**, p. **47**

Reed, S. 2015, 'Kim Kardashian Says the Darndest Things: Her 25 Best Quotes', *The Hollywood Reporter* (online), www.hollywoodreporter.com – p. **19**

Saini, M. 2010 'Kim Kardashian Powering to the Top', *Forbes* (online), www.forbes.com – p. **52**

Sandberg, P. 2012, 'Reality Check: Kim Kardashian on Kanye West and Privacy in a Public Life', *V Magazine* (online), www.vmagazine.com – p. **57**

Talarico, B. 2014, 'Kylie Jenner Says Her Style "Changes Every Month," Plus, See Kendall's New Haircut!', *People* (online), www.people.com – p. **18**

The Late Show with David Letterman, 2013 – p. **84**

Van Meter, J. 2018, 'Kendall Jenner Gets Candid About Her Career, Her Controversies and Her Private Life', *Vogue* (online), www.vogue.com – p. **53**

Wallace, C. 2015, 'Kylie Jenner', *Interview* (online), www.interviewmagazine.com – p. **75**

Warwick, C. 2015, 'The 11 Best Quotes from Kim Kardashian's Powerful Speech at the Commonwealth Club', MTV (online), www.mtv.co.uk – p. **16**

Pocket Kardashian Wisdom

Published in 2019 by Hardie Grant Books,
an imprint of Hardie Grant Publishing

Hardie Grant Books (London)
5th & 6th Floors
52–54 Southwark Street
London SE1 1UN

Hardie Grant Books (Melbourne)
Building 1, 658 Church Street
Richmond, Victoria 3121

hardiegrantbooks.com

British Library Cataloguing-in-Publication Data. A catalogue record for this
book is available from the British Library.

ISBN: 978-1-78488-286-0

Publishing Director: Kate Pollard
Junior Editor: Rebecca Fitzsimons
Designer: Studio Noel
Illustrator: Michele Rosenthal

Colour Reproduction by p2d
Printed and bound in China by Leo Paper Group

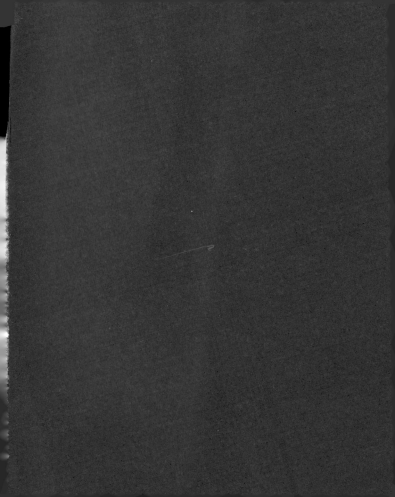